WOODROW WILSON

ENCYCLOPEDIA
of PRESIDENTS

Woodrow Wilson

Twenty-Eighth President of the United States

By Alice Osinski

Consultant: Charles Abele, Ph.D.
Social Studies Instructor
Chicago Public School System

 CHILDRENS PRESS ®
CHICAGO

Wilson rides to his 1913 inauguration with outgoing president William Howard Taft.

Library of Congress Cataloging-in-Publication Data

Osinski, Alice.
    Woodrow Wilson / by Alice Osinski
        p.   cm. — (Encyclopedia of presidents)
    Includes index.
    Summary: Follows the life and career of the scholar and
educator who was president of the United States during World
War I.
    ISBN 0-516-01367-X
    1.   Wilson, Woodrow, 1856-1924—Juvenile
literature.   2.   Presidents—United States—Biography—
Juvenile literature.   3.   World War, 1914-1918—Juvenile
literature.   [1.   Wilson, Woodrow, 1856-
1924.   2.   Presidents.]   I.   Title.   II.   Series.
E767.093   1989   88-8678
973.91′3′0924—dc19   CIP
[B]   [92]   AC

Picture Acknowledgments

AP/Wide World Photos—6, 32, 57, 69 (top left),
75, 82

The Bettmann Archive Inc.—4, 5, 8, 9, 43 (top),
46, 48, 50 (2 pictures), 53, 54, 58, 65, 68, 69
(top right and bottom), 71, 72, 76, 78 (bottom),
79, 80, 81, 84, 86

Bryn Mawr College—30

The Ferdinand Hamburger, Jr. Archives, The
Johns Hopkins University—26, 27

Historical Pictures Service, Chicago— 28, 31, 42,
60, 66, 67, 70, 73, 78 (top)

Library of Congress—38, 47, 49, 50, 62, 89

Manuscripts Print Collection, Special Collections
Department, University of Virginia Library—21

National Portrait Gallery, Smithsonian
Institution, Washington, D.C.—44

North Wind Picture Archives—36

Princeton University Library—13 (2 pictures),
18, 22, 24, 25, 33, 34, 35, 37, 43 (bottom)

U.S. Bureau of Printing and Engraving—2

Woodrow Wilson Birthplace Foundation—10, 12
(2 pictures), 14, 16

Cover design and illustration
by Steven Gaston Dobson

Woodrow Wilson in August 1912
after his nomination for the
presidency at the Democratic
national convention in Baltimore

Table of Contents

American infantrymen in France during World War I

Chapter 1

Rendezvous with War

Day dawned wet and hazy on the Western Front of the great war in Europe. It was March 1917, and French soldiers, hiding in well-worn trenches, peered out over the barren wasteland called No Man's Land. Seconds later, several small explosions shattered the silence. Caught by surprise, the men watched in horror as a sickly, greenish-white mist rose from the smoke and drifted toward them. Within minutes they were covered by it.

The soldiers panicked, frantically reaching for their gas masks to protect their burning eyes and throats from the poisonous gas. For many of them it was too late. Overcome by the pain, and unable to see or breathe well, they lay defenseless before the approaching German army.

Thousands of miles away, President Woodrow Wilson was sitting in the Oval Office of the White House in Washington, D.C., typing a speech he would soon deliver before Congress. He had never looked so worn, and he had never faced such a difficult task. In a few days, he would ask Congress to declare war on Germany.

American troops with gas masks—and one without—in France

"Once lead this people [America] into war," he told a friend, "and they'll forget there ever was such a thing as tolerance. To fight you must be brutal and ruthless, and the spirit of ruthless brutality will enter into the very fiber of our national life, infecting Congress, the courts, the policeman on the beat, the man in the street."

Earlier Wilson had confided to a friend that "for nights he'd been lying awake going over the whole situation; over the provocation given by Germany, over the probable feeling in the United States, over the consequences . . . to the world at large" if the United States were to enter the war. He believed that he had tried every way to avoid war but that he was now left with no alternative.

Rubbing his tired, burning eyes, the president rose from his chair and went to the window. Peering out, he cleared his throat and began practicing the speech that would change the direction of history. "The world must be

Allied soldiers advance up a hill amidst smoke and rubble.

made safe for democracy," he cried. "Towards this endeavor and for the things we Americans hold nearest our hearts, we are willing to shed our blood—for democracy, for the right of those who submit to authority to have a voice in their own Governments, for the rights and liberties of small nations. . . ."

The president's voice rose to a persuasive pitch. "To such a task we can dedicate . . . everything that we are and everything that we have, with the pride of those who know that the day has come when America is privileged to spend her blood and her might for the principles that gave her birth and happiness and the peace which she has treasured. God helping her, she can do no other."

At the conclusion of his speech, Wilson collapsed into his chair, exhausted. Holding his head in his trembling hands, he sighed. How could he ever resolve the mounting problems the war would bring?

The Presbyterian Church in Staunton, Virginia

Chapter 2

Like Father, Like Son

Most people in Staunton, Virginia, were still celebrating Christmas when Thomas Woodrow Wilson was born on December 29, 1856. His parents, Joseph Ruggles Wilson and Jessie Woodrow Wilson, both of Scotch-Irish ancestry, were proud of their son.

Tommy was almost two years old when his family moved to Augusta, Georgia. His father, a Presbyterian minister, had become pastor of Augusta's First Presbyterian Church. At the time, Augusta was a small, quiet town surrounded by fine plantations in the heart of the Old South. The First Presbyterian Church, standing prominently in the center of the town, was attended by the most influential and wealthy members of the community.

Two years after the Wilson family moved to Augusta, the Civil War broke out between the states. Although Tommy was only four years old then, he remembered hearing people talk about it. "My earliest recollection," he said, "was standing at my father's gateway . . . when I was four years old, and hearing someone pass and say that Mr. Lincoln was elected and there was to be war."

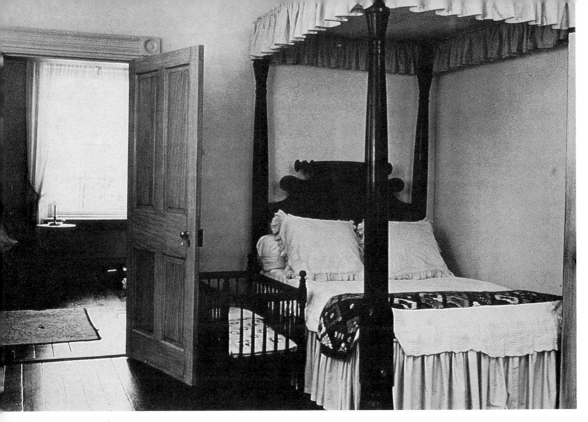

Woodrow Wilson's birthplace in Staunton, Virginia: His parents' bedroom with his crib beside the bed (above) and the home's exterior, overlooking a garden

Joseph Ruggles Wilson and Janet Woodrow Wilson

When the war began, Augusta became one of the main munitions centers for the Confederate army. Mr. Wilson, a loyal Southerner, served as an army chaplain and allowed his church to be used as a Confederate hospital and prison.

Curious about soldiers, Tommy often would sneak over to the church to watch his father care for the wounded. Captured Union soldiers were being held in the churchyard, and Tommy would pretend to stand guard from a nearby hideout. Many years later, when he was president of the United States, he would relive these memories as he agonized over his decision to send American soldiers to fight the great war in Europe.

Tommy's sisters, Anne and Marion

Although war raged all about them, Mr. and Mrs. Wilson managed to maintain a happy home life. They showered their four children—Marion, Anne, Thomas, and Joseph, Jr.—with love and affection. Daily they would gather in the family room to sing, pray, and read aloud. Among their favorite books were those by Sir Walter Scott and Charles Dickens. In this atmosphere of books and storytelling, Tommy's talents flourished.

He did not learn the alphabet until he was nine and had not mastered the basics of reading until the age of eleven. However, Tommy could speak well on almost any topic. His father had taught him to develop this skill.

14

Every Sunday afternoon they would sit and have a talk. Tommy seemed to absorb all his father's spoken thoughts and behavior. He idolized his father, saying often that he was "the best instructor, the most inspiring companion . . . that a youngster ever had."

On Mondays they would go on excursions into the city or the neighboring countryside to learn firsthand how some particular invention or process worked. Later they would talk over the experience, his father insisting that every idea Tommy expressed be in perfect English. As Tommy grew older, his father would read a passage aloud from a favorite author, and they would pick it apart to see how the ideas could be expressed better.

Mr. Wilson continued to teach Tommy until he left for college. His influence continued throughout his son's life. A famous historian once said that "until after he was forty years old, Woodrow Wilson never made an important decision of any kind without first seeking his father's advice."

In 1870, when Tommy was thirteen, he and his family moved to Columbia, South Carolina. There Mr. Wilson took a position as professor in the Presbyterian Theological Seminary. At the time Columbia was just emerging from the ashes of the Civil War and struggling to survive. The Wilsons bought a plot of land on Hampton Street with money they had saved during the war. On it they built one of the finest houses in the town.

Tommy was enrolled in a private school. Although he was popular with his classmates, according to one biographer, some of them thought "he was not like the other boys. He had a queer way of going off by himself."

The Wilsons' home in Columbia, South Carolina

When Mr. Wilson began to teach at the seminary, Tommy attended his lectures. He wanted to be just like his father, whom he admired as the finest minister in the world. Often Tommy would be found curled up in an alcove in the library, reading to prepare for the ministry.

When not accompanying his father somewhere, or reading in the library, Tommy was organizing his friends into one kind of club or another. If it wasn't baseball, then it was the Light Foots, a club over which he was president. He wrote a constitution for the club and conducted meetings using parliamentary procedure. Even as a youngster, he was interested in seeing how people could be organized, which were the best rules for holding them together, and what were the best ways to lead them.

In the fall of 1873, Tommy enrolled at Davidson College in North Carolina to study for the Presbyterian ministry. Almost seventeen, he was anxious to follow in his father's footsteps. But Tommy was poorly prepared for college. Although he did well in English and composition, he found great difficulty with mathematics and Greek. By the end of the year, he had achieved only average grades. Young Wilson's failure to achieve perfection led him to the verge of a physical breakdown. In June he returned home in ill health. The pressures of school took such a toll on him that even the family butler remarked that Tommy looked like "an old young man."

For the next fifteen months, the tall, awkward eighteen-year-old spent his days reading, thinking, and dreaming. From time to time he would poke around the docks of Wilmington, North Carolina, where his family had recently moved, and watch visiting ships from foreign countries. There too, under a favorite tree, Tommy sometimes sat with a friend to discuss the meaning of a story they had taken turns reading aloud.

Though he had been dissatisfied with his grades at Davidson College, Tommy had made an important discovery that year. He realized that he was more interested in politics than in the ministry. As a member of Davidson's debating team, he had seen his leadership abilities and skills as a persuasive speaker emerge. He had found it thrilling to express his opinions on such difficult topics as, "Was the introduction of slavery in the United States beneficial to the human race?" or "Was the death of Lincoln beneficial to the South?"

Chapter 3

Promising Orator

In September 1875, after more than a year at home, Tommy enrolled at Princeton University in New Jersey to study politics. One morning, carrying only his father's old black bag, he walked into the school, determined to make these the best years of his life. Once again, however, Tommy was poorly prepared. His grades never matched what he expected of himself. Although never one of the best students in the school, it was said that many looked up to him as "one of the most original and superior men at the college."

He soon gained a reputation as the school's best debater and won the highest honor of the Whig Society. This was a famous debating club organized by James Madison in 1769. Tommy was admired for his original thinking and for the brilliant way in which he communicated his ideas and persuaded others to agree with him. Being able to think original thoughts, and have those thoughts influence the thinking of others, was at the heart of who Woodrow Wilson was.

Opposite page: Wilson's 1879 Princeton class picture

Wilson once wrote to a friend: "The man who reads everything is like the man who eats everything: he can digest nothing; and the penalty for cramming one's mind with other men's thoughts is to have no thoughts of one's own. Only that which enables one to do his own thinking is of real value."

Young Wilson used every spare moment to polish his speaking techniques and practice the famous speeches of such men as Patrick Henry and Daniel Webster. He practiced wherever he could, whether alone in the woods near the university or in his father's empty church during his visits home. Whatever it took to develop his power as a public speaker, he was willing to do.

As Tommy's knowledge of politics expanded, so too did his ability to express himself in writing. Teachers read his essays with enthusiasm, marveling at his grasp of world affairs and his ability to present fresh, clear ideas. One of his better-known articles, "Cabinet Government in the United States," was expanded later into a book.

An intense student and a likable fellow, young Wilson became managing editor of the *Princetonian* and the central figure in a campus discussion group known as the Witherspoon Gang. His personal charm attracted many people. He sang and danced well, told wonderful stories, and was kind and considerate to less able students. When he graduated in June 1879, he had a small following of devoted friends and admirers.

Although Tommy returned to Wilmington after graduation, he stayed only a short while. Intending to launch a career in politics, he went back to school—this time to

Wilson (left) with fellow members of the Jefferson Society, also called the Jeff

study law. Young Wilson knew that he had the gift of leadership. He knew he possessed an unusual grasp of history and politics and was an outstanding orator and debater. To gain entrance to public office, however, what he lacked was a background in law.

In October, Wilson entered the University of Virginia law school in Charlottesville. Besides taking a full load of classes, he joined the debating society and won its award for best orator. The following report appeared in the October 1880 issue of the university magazine: "The delivery of this medal to the Gladstone-like speaker of the University elicited one of the clearest, soundest, most logical, and thoroughly sensible addresses ever pronounced here at the University by a man so young. It was head and shoulders above the average efforts of college men, and won the applause of persons highly capable of passing an impartial judgment."

Wilson developed his public speaking skills during his college days.
Above: Wilson as the orator for Princeton's 150th anniversary in 1896

Wilson's extracurricular activities soon began piling up on his law courses. It all proved too much for him. In frail health, he was forced to leave school halfway through his second year. Everyone regretted Tommy's leaving, for he was genuinely liked and admired—a natural leader. Discouraged, he returned home wondering, "How [could] a man with a weak body . . . ever arrive anywhere?"

Wilson spent the next year and a half in lonely but intense study, practicing speeches every day. Around this time he dropped the name Tommy and began using his middle name, Woodrow.

In the spring of 1882 he felt well enough to venture out on his own. At age twenty-five, he moved to Atlanta, Georgia, and looked up a friend, Edward Renick. Both highly gifted and intensely interested in books, the two decided to practice law together. Although Woodrow would not be admitted to the bar until October, he and Renick became law partners and opened an office on the second floor of an old building.

While waiting for clients, Wilson kept up his reading on history and politics and began buying books to fill up the bookcase he had bought when he was at Princeton. Rather than borrow from the library, he liked to buy books. That way, he could put his name in each of them and write notes in the margins.

On October 19, 1882, Wilson was admitted to the bar and permitted to practice law in Georgia state courts. The following March he qualified to practice in the federal courts.

However, business failed to pick up for the firm of Wilson and Renick. For extra income, Wilson began writing articles for the *New York Evening Post*.

Soon Wilson came to realize that a law practice was not for him:

"Whoever thinks, as I thought, that he can practice law successfully and study history and politics at the same time is woefully mistaken. If he is to make a living at the bar he must be a lawyer and nothing else." A career in politics was still Wilson's highest ambition, but now he knew that he would have to reach it in some other way. He decided to go back to school.

Ellen Louise Axson
around the time of
her engagement

In April 1883, while visiting his uncle in Rome,
Georgia, Woodrow met Ellen Louise Axson and began
courting her. The pretty twenty-three-year-old, said a
relative, "had a flower-like appearance; her hair was a
bronze gold, her eyes were a deep brown, and her face was
all aglow with the marvellous colour that she never lost."

Ellen's interests were similar to Woodrow's, and her
aspirations were just as high. Like him, she had grown up
in a home filled with books. It might also be said that, like
him, she was an artist — she painted pictures with a
paintbrush, while Woodrow painted them with words.

After a fast and furious courtship, the two were
engaged. Although very much in love, both agreed to complete their studies before getting married. Woodrow began

Wilson as a young lawyer in Atlanta around 1882

his graduate school studies in history, economics, and political science at Johns Hopkins University in Baltimore, Maryland. Ellen enrolled at an art school in New York.

While they were apart, Woodrow wrote lengthy letters to Ellen, sharing all his thoughts and activities with her. In one letter he confided, "You are the only person in the world without any exception—to whom I can tell all that my heart contains." For Woodrow, there was plenty to tell.

He threw himself into his studies at Johns Hopkins, yet he still had time for extra activities. He joined the choir, helped organize a glee club, and spoke at a number of social gatherings. After reorganizing the debating society, he wrote a new constitution for the literary society.

Wilson (back row, second from left) with the Johns Hopkins University Glee Club

In addition to taking a full load of classes and participating in other university activities, Woodrow wrote his first book, *Congressional Government*. Published in 1885, it was an immediate success. Eventually, it would be translated into several languages and go through twenty-nine editions.

Woodrow sent the first copy of his book to Ellen. "In sending you my first book, darling," he wrote, "I renew the gift of myself." He sent a second copy to his father, in the dedication calling him the "patient guide of his youth, gracious companion of his manhood, his best instructor and most lenient critic. . . ."

The history and politics seminar room at Johns Hopkins, where Wilson studied

Everything Woodrow attempted at Johns Hopkins seemed to succeed. Still, Ellen knew he wasn't satisfied. In one of his letters to her he spoke of something missing in his life—something, he said, upon which "both my gifts and inclinations gave me a claim; I do feel a very real regret that I have been shut out of my heart's first—primary—ambition and purpose, which was, to take an active, if possible a leading, part in public life, and strike out for myself, if I had the ability, a statesman's career. That is my heart's, —or, rather, my mind's—deepest secret. . . ."

Unfortunately, he saw no opportunity to get into public office himself. So, for the time being, he turned his attentions to teaching, lecturing, and writing.

Bryn Mawr College in Bryn Mawr, Pennsylvania

Chapter 4

Teacher, Writer, Lecturer

In 1885 Bryn Mawr College was being organized in Bryn Mawr, Pennsylvania. It was the first college in the United States to offer women a graduate education comparable to that being offered to men. Looking for "outstanding young men of the country" to organize its various departments, the college contacted Wilson and offered him a position as a history teacher. Against Ellen's wishes, Woodrow accepted and left Johns Hopkins before completing his degree. Later he submitted his published book, *Congressional Government*, as his thesis, took the examinations, and received his doctor of philosophy (Ph.D.) degree.

When Ellen returned from her art studies in New York, she and Woodrow were married. The following September they moved to Pennsylvania and settled down at Bryn Mawr College, where Woodrow plunged into his work. Immediately he began ordering books, preparing courses, and writing lectures in ancient and modern history.

Wilson (in doorway, far right) with Bryn Mawr graduating class

His classes were popular among the students. One said: "His lectures were fascinating and held me spellbound; each was an almost perfect essay in itself, well rounded and with a distinct literary style. Never have I known a mind that could reason so profoundly and so clearly, with such breadth of vision."

But soon the challenge and excitement of setting up a new school began to wear off. Woodrow felt limited by his surroundings and unfulfilled by teaching women. The salary was barely enough to support two, and now Ellen was expecting a baby. To make additional money and calm his restless spirit, Wilson began writing essays for the *Atlantic Monthly* and developing his ideas for a new book. Not long after their baby, Margaret, was born, he began a series of twenty-five lectures at Johns Hopkins. The Wilsons welcomed the extra income, for in the summer of 1887 their second child, Jessie, was born.

The library at Wesleyan University

By his third year at Bryn Mawr, Wilson was becoming increasingly impatient and unhappy. At thirty-one he felt as if his life were standing still. Because he was anxious and overworked, his health began to fail. "I almost fear I shall break down in health here if I stay another year," he told Ellen.

So when an offer came in 1888 to teach at Wesleyan University in Connecticut at a much higher salary, he accepted. He was delighted to be teaching men, and he showed great enthusiasm in everything that he did. "Every man in his class," said one of his students, "felt inspired to do his very best, not because of any exhortation or threat, or even suggestion, from Wilson himself, but from the very atmosphere of his personality; not a feeling of fear or consequences was present, but a feeling that you were ashamed if you were not at your best."

Wilson (front, third from left) with the Wesleyan faculty in 1889

Wilson was happy teaching at Wesleyan. As coach of the football team, he developed it into one of the finest teams in the school's history. Having more time to write and a well-equipped library to use, he also was able to finish another book, *The State*. That same year, 1889, a third daughter, Eleanor, was born.

The Wilsons spent two wonderful years at Wesleyan. They would have stayed longer if it had not been for another job offer that came Woodrow's way—one that he simply couldn't refuse.

In 1890 Wilson was offered a teaching position at Princeton University. As a student he had been happy there. Now he was overjoyed at the prospect of returning as a professor of law and political economy. Gladly he accepted the position.

Ellen Wilson at Princeton in 1891

In September, he, Ellen, and their three daughters moved into a comfortable, roomy, frame house, only a short walk from the university buildings. As Ellen settled the family in, Woodrow began preparing for his classes. His lecture room, one of the largest in the university, accommodated more than four hundred students. In some of his courses, every seat would be taken.

From the very beginning Wilson had a powerful influence on the students. Many of them considered him the greatest classroom lecturer they had ever heard. It was not uncommon for them to cheer him at the end of his lectures. Year after year they voted him most popular professor.

Margaret Wilson (age five) and Jessie Wilson (age four)

Eleanor Wilson (age three)

Princeton University, where Wilson taught from 1890 until 1902

Wilson was popular among the faculty members, too. When asked to describe his influences on the faculty, one member replied, "He led us . . . by his wit, his incisive questioning mind, his courage, and his preeminence in faculty debates."

But Princeton matters were not the only ones that absorbed Wilson's time. He wrote another book, *Division and Reunion*, and continued writing journal articles. Besides teaching at Princeton, he lectured at Johns Hopkins University and other schools and delivered speeches throughout the United States. At least seven major universities offered him the position of president of their school.

Wilson at the time of his election as Princeton's president

Wilson's work load and his intensity began to take their toll. Before the close of the 1896 school year, he was near exhaustion. Suffering from a severe case of neuritis (inflammation of the nerves), he lost the use of his right hand. Upon the advice of his doctor, he sailed to Europe for a long rest. The summer abroad gave him time to recover. When he returned to Princeton, he resumed writing and lecturing harder than ever.

In 1900, after six years of teaching at Princeton, he considered the idea of devoting all his time to his own writing. He asked the university for a one-year leave of absence. But before he could carry out his plan, he was elected president of the university.

Chapter 5

On to Princeton!

On June 9, 1902, Wilson was unanimously elected president of Princeton. He was the first president in Princeton's history who was not a clergyman. An impressive inaugural celebration followed. Among those attending were notable educators, authors, statesmen, and businessmen. Never before had there been such a distinguished gathering of celebrities for a college ceremony. Yet, of all those attending, Wilson was most proud of having his father there. He did not know that, three months later, his father would be dead.

Those who had elected Wilson as president believed that he would bring new life to the university. Wilson did that and more. Surpassing all their expectations, he drastically changed Princeton's reputation in the academic world.

The first thing he did was to get more donations for the school. Then, ignoring opposition, he changed the kinds of courses being offered and the manner in which they were being taught. Next he asked the board of directors for more professors and new laboratories and dormitories. He found some of the ablest men in the country to head the departments. Many were attracted by his idealism and the fresh new spirit of his leadership.

As Princeton's reputation for excellence spread, Wilson became even more dedicated and involved. But early in 1905 his health began to decline. Ignoring his weakening condition, he continued his fast pace and even increased his lecturing throughout the country. Speaking on political issues of the day, he began making converts and followers wherever he went. One historian commented: "Here was a man with no political background whatever, no political experience, no political friends, no political organization, and yet people were beginning to think of him and suggest him for president of the United States. It was the sheer, unaided power and personality of the man."

By May of the following year, Wilson was suffering from neuritis of the left shoulder and leg. In great pain, he had partial use of only one hand and lost the vision in his left eye. Doctors advised him to give up his demanding career, retire, and lead a quiet life. Refusing to quit his life-style altogether, Wilson took the summer to recover at a country cottage in England with his family. He returned to Princeton in October, much improved and prepared to send the manuscript for a new book, *Constitutional Government*, to his publisher.

Wilson's power and prestige were growing. People admired his direct approach to the country's problems and the manner in which he stood up for what he believed. Soon people began thinking of him as a politician. In 1909, after he delivered a commencement address at Princeton, *Harper's Weekly* stated, "We now expect to see Woodrow Wilson elected Governor of the State of New Jersey in 1910 and nominated president in 1912. . . ."

Although everything seemed to be going right for Wilson outside of Princeton, turmoil within the university was seriously threatening his leadership.

Princeton had a graduate school but did not have separate buildings to house it. Believing that the graduate college should be an intimate part of the university, Wilson suggested that new buildings be constructed on campus. "We shall build it," he said, "not apart, but as nearly as may be at the very heart . . . of the university."

Graduate school dean Andrew West and his supporters disagreed with Wilson. They believed that it should be housed in separate buildings off campus. Soon they were involved in a heated battle. More fuel was added to the fire when a wealthy graduate of the college donated $500,000 for the new graduate school buildings and said that they had to be built off campus. Soon the controversy spilled over into the press. Wilson, feeling he would gain more support for his side if he brought this problem to the public, conducted a cross-country speaking tour to explain his ideas. The question he posed was: Should the wealthy and privileged who donate money to the university have the right to make major decisions regarding it?

As Wilson debated the issue, he seemed to be gaining support. But then another wealthy graduate of Princeton died, leaving everything he owned to Princeton's graduate school. When Dean West became one of the trustees of the estate, Wilson knew he had lost the fight. "We have beaten the living," he sarcastically told Ellen, "but we cannot fight the dead. The game is up." On June 9, 1910, the university trustees accepted West's plans.

Wilson visiting with Princeton students after he became president

Wilson now realized that he could not continue working in an environment that did not support his goals. On September 15, he was officially nominated as the Democratic candidate for governor of New Jersey. Welcoming this opportunity to get into politics, he resigned as president of Princeton in October.

Leaving Princeton, however, would not be easy. He admitted: "For many years I have been preaching to the young men of Princeton that it was their duty to give service to the public and take their part in political affairs. This nomination has been handed to me upon a silver platter and I am under no obligations of any shape, manner, or form to anybody. I hate like poison to leave this place but I could not refuse."

Right: Wilson walking through the Princeton campus in his academic robes

Below: "Prospect," the house on campus where Wilson lived when he was president of Princeton

FOR GOVERNOR

WOODROW WILSON

Chapter 6

Eloquent Statesman

Margaret, Jessie, and Eleanor Wilson took turns singing the verses of an old Presbyterian hymn as they unpacked the neatly stacked boxes in the hallway of the modest house on Cleveland Lane. The family had moved there shortly after Mr. Wilson was nominated for governor.

It was important that the family help him campaign. After all, he had no real political connections in New Jersey before becoming a candidate. He had not come up through the ranks as most candidates had done. And he was not a typical professional politician, successful businessman, or lawyer.

Influential party boss James Smith, Jr., and his friend George Harvey backed Wilson because they believed they could control him. They and others hoped to take advantage of his lack of political training. But Wilson showed that he was a new type of political leader. His fresh, honest ideas appealed to voters. After an exhausting tour of speech making and hand shaking, he was elected by a landslide in November 1910 as the forty-third governor of New Jersey.

Sea Girt, New Jersey, Wilson's home

No one but the politicians who had backed him doubted that Wilson would keep his campaign promises. During his term as governor, he passed a law allowing voters to nominate and elect all candidates for public office—even U.S. senators and delegates to the national party conventions. He set up government regulations to protect citizens from unfair rate charges by trolley, gas, electric, telephone, and telegraph companies. Finally, he proposed a fair and honest employers' liability and compensation act. Under this act, if an employee were injured or killed while on the job, the employer would be obligated to help him or his family financially.

Opposite page: Wilson running for
New Jersey governor in 1911

Wilson giving a speech after his nomination for the presidency

Wilson had little carefree time and not much of a private life during his hectic years as governor. But he accomplished a great deal. His reform measures changed New Jersey from a conservative state to a progressive one. Democrats were impressed with his accomplishments. Many believed he should run for president of the United States in 1912.

Much political maneuvering went on during the Democratic national convention in June 1912. Wilson was nominated as the party's candidate for president on the forty-sixth ballot. Now he would have to prove that he could win the election. Most Democrats believed that he

The Wilson family at Sea Girt in 1912

would win. The Republicans' loyalties were badly split, with Conservative Republicans supporting President William Howard Taft and Progressive Republicans nominating former president Theodore Roosevelt.

As Ellen and the girls settled in at the Governor's Cottage at Sea Girt on the Jersey coast, Wilson gave his first campaign speech from the front porch. He knew he would be competing against the exciting and forceful personality of Teddy Roosevelt, so his promises had to be more attractive. Gradually, he came up with the idea of calling his program the "New Freedom" for the "man who is knocking and fighting at the doors of opportunity."

Theodore Roosevelt delivering a campaign speech

As the weeks passed, the campaign turned into a series of political debates between Wilson and Roosevelt. The debates were as rousing as any since the Abraham Lincoln-Stephen Douglas debates of 1858. Wilson, always at his best when debating, called for "freedom from control by a select group of wealthy people.... [I am] against the powers that have governed us," he cried, "that have limited our development—that have determined our lives—that have set us in a straitjacket to do as they please.... The treasury of America does not lie in the brains of the small body of men now in control of the great enterprises that have been concentrated under the direction of a small number of persons."

Above: Wilson campaigning for the presidency
Below: A "women's campaign" for Woodrow Wilson

Wilson's direct, honest, and eloquent manner of speaking inspired his listeners. He loved the crowds and actually seemed to thrive on the physical rigors of the campaign. After delivering his last speech in New York City, he returned home to await election results.

On November 5, 1912, the Wilson family and a small circle of friends gathered in his living room to listen to the election returns. At ten o'clock, after Wilson had retired to his room, Ellen brought him the news of his election as twenty-eighth president of the United States. He carried only 42 percent of the popular vote. But because the Republicans were split between Roosevelt and Taft, he won a smashing victory in the electoral college, taking 435 of the 531 electoral votes.

As news of Wilson's victory spread, the bells at Princeton University tolled. Students holding a torchlight parade surrounded his home and persuaded him to come out. Responding to his first request as president, Wilson walked out in front of them. Managing to control his shaking voice, he stood up on a chair and asked the crowd to dedicate their lives to "[setting the] government forward by processes of justice, equity and fairness." For himself, he added, "I . . . have no feeling of triumph tonight. I have a feeling of solemn responsibility."

A week and a half later, Wilson and his family were sailing for Bermuda. "I find myself, after two years of continuous strain, rather completely fagged out," he told a friend. Wilson knew that if he did not take time to rest and prepare for the tasks ahead of him, he would never be able to cope with the problems of his new office.

The Wilson family at home around the fireplace in 1913

Chapter 7

The Promise of a
New Freedom

As president of the United States, Woodrow Wilson was determined to administer government honestly and without favor to individuals or classes. To achieve the New Freedom he had promised in his campaign, Wilson sought reforms in three major areas: tariffs, banking, and trade.

Breaking with the tradition set by President Thomas Jefferson, Wilson appeared before Congress to deliver his requests in person. On April 8, 1913, he addressed Congress on the important issue of tariffs, or import taxes, that benefited a few large companies. "We must abolish everything that bears even the semblance of privilege or of any kind of artificial advantage," he said, "and [make] businessmen and producers efficient, economical, and enterprising masters of competitive supremacy, better workers and merchants than any in the world."

When Congress passed the Underwood Tariff Act in October, Wilson was thrilled and even confessed: "I have had the accomplishment of something like this at heart ever since I was a boy."

In June Wilson presented his program to revise the banking and currency systems, which were unsafe and out of date. He proposed setting up the Federal Reserve System, which consisted of a board of directors and twelve banks holding deposits in reserve. Wilson believed that this would stabilize money and credit throughout the country. In December, the Federal Reserve Act was passed.

Next Wilson created the Federal Trade Commission to enforce fair trade practices. Next he signed the Clayton Antitrust Act, which would curb unfair practices of big business.

In foreign affairs, resolving problems became more complicated. Relations between the United States and Japan and China were strained, and a conflict in the Panama Canal Zone needed attention. But Wilson's most difficult crisis was in Mexico, where vital American interests were at stake.

For several years, Mexico had been involved in a civil war. In 1913 Victoriano Huerta seized power, had the previous president killed, and set up a dictatorship. Angered by Huerta's methods, Wilson denounced his regime and vowed to destroy it. After Huerta's troops arrested fourteen Americans in Mexico, Wilson sent marines to occupy the Mexican port of Veracruz. Intending to cut off supplies from reaching Huerta's army, eighteen marines were killed.

Later, in 1914, the United States helped Mexican revolutionaries, led by Venustiano Carranza, to force Huerta out of the country. After Huerta fled, other revolutionaries began fighting among themselves. Pancho Villa

Mexican general Emiliano Zapata

and Emiliano Zapata, wanting more reforms than Carranza would give them, led their armies in revolt. Because the United States supported Carranza, Pancho Villa crossed the Mexican border in 1916 and raided Columbus, New Mexico. Eighteen Americans died in the skirmish.

Immediately Wilson sent troops under General John J. Pershing to pursue Villa into Mexico. But Villa was never captured. Eventually, Carranza was recognized as Mexico's president and the conflict was temporarily resolved.

Considering world affairs at the time, the crisis in Mexico was only a small conflict compared to the enormous war raging in Europe.

Chapter 8

"A War to End All Wars"

Edward House, Wilson's top aide, looked in through the half-open door of the oval office. The president was at his desk, deep in thought.

"Mr. President," he said, as he walked into the stuffy room, "have you read the morning paper—the article on the build-up of European armies?"

"Yes," the president gravely replied. "Something has to be done."

When Woodrow Wilson began his first term of office in 1913, European nations were teetering on the brink of war. Over the past forty years the populations of England, France, Russia, and Austria-Hungary had doubled in size. Their industries and armies had expanded, and they had increased their land holdings. Germany and Italy were eager to do the same.

As these countries competed for trade markets and overseas colonies, suspicions and rivalries developed. Nations began forming alliances to protect themselves. By 1914 there were two major alliances in Europe. One was called the Triple Alliance (the Central Powers). It was made up of Germany, Austria-Hungary, and Italy. Italy later left the alliance but was replaced by the Ottoman Empire (Turkey and Bulgaria today). The other alliance, called the Triple Entente (the Allied Powers or the Allies), was made up of France, Russia, and Great Britain.

Archduke Francis Ferdinand (left) arriving in Sarajevo with his wife

Hoping to end the tensions building in Europe, Wilson sent Edward House to resolve some of the differences. His first order of business was to propose a pact of friendship among England, Germany, and the United States. But no agreements came from his peace mission. He returned to the United States with news that the entire European continent was braced for war, waiting for an event to set it off.

On June 28, 1914, that dreaded event occurred. Archduke Francis Ferdinand, heir to the throne of Austria-Hungary, and his wife were shot and killed by a Serbian patriot while visiting Sarajevo, in Bosnia (now in Yugoslavia). Tensions had been building in Bosnia, where people resented being ruled by Austria-Hungary.

Suspecting that Serbia had approved of the plot to assassinate the archduke, Austria-Hungary declared war. Immediately Russia came to Serbia's aid. Germany, angered by Russia's support of Serbia, declared war on both of them on August 1. The same day, France readied its army to support Russia. Two days later Germany declared war on France and invaded neutral Belgium. Then on August 4 England declared war on Germany. Thus, within a matter of days, all of Europe was involved in war.

Although many Americans sided with the Allied powers in the war, few of them wanted the United States to become involved. Since there was no threat to American lives or property, why should they be drawn into a war three thousand miles away?

President Wilson had no intention of entering the war. He stated that America would remain neutral; it would not take sides. "Our whole duty for the present, at any rate," he said, "is summed up in the motto America First: Let us think of America before we think of Europe."

But as Americans in business and finance began pressuring him to support the Allies, President Wilson had to compromise. Private banking firms asked for permission to loan money to the Allies. American farmers and manufacturers began to protest restrictions on trade with them. Before long, Wilson had to allow Americans the opportunity to sell goods and loan money to any foreign country.

As U.S. exports of wheat and munitions soared, however, it was becoming more and more difficult for America to remain neutral.

Ellen Wilson, who died in 1914

Foreign concerns were not the only problems weighing heavily on the president's mind. There were personal ones as well. During the summer of 1913 Ellen was diagnosed as having nephritis, a kidney disease. She was given little time to live. Several months later, after a fall, her condition worsened. The president began spending every spare moment at her bedside. Then on August 6, 1914, he cancelled all of his appointments so that he could be with her when she died.

Devastated by Ellen's death, Wilson broke down, sobbing. How could he ever live without her? She was the only person who had understood him and his needs. She had guided him at every turn. To whom could he open his heart now that she was gone?

As Wilson was recovering from his loss, European leaders were mobilizing for war. Certain that the fighting would be over by autumn, enthusiastic crowds cheered their armies as they marched off to fight. In France, troops were accompanied by brass bands and waving flags. Officers wearing colorfully plumed helmets and white gloves rode by on horses, as red- and blue-uniformed foot soldiers followed in columns. None of them had any idea they would be fighting against tanks, machine guns, flame throwers, and poisonous gas.

At the outbreak of the war, Germany and France had the largest armies. Germany, realizing that the Allies had superior navies, planned to defeat them on land. Germany intended to win a quick victory by knocking France out of the war early and then turning on Russia.

France's strategy was to halt Germany's invasion of Belgium, push back the enemy lines, and take the German capital of Berlin. Russians believed they could defeat Austria-Hungary and then move on into Germany. For their part, the Austrians planned to occupy Serbia. And Great Britain intended to defeat Germany by blockading its ports, thereby preventing supplies from getting in. None of these plans worked out as they were intended, however.

The French army stopped the Germans at the Marne River, just fifteen miles from Paris. The two sides dug trenches to protect some of their troops, while additional armies raced toward the sea. They intended to outflank each other along the way and cut through each other's lines. But neither side was successful.

Instead, what each side did was to build a system of trenches, nearly five hundred miles in length, from the English Channel to the border of Switzerland. Called the Western Front, the two opposing systems of trenches faced each other and brought the war to a standstill.

As 1915 dawned, about two million Germans faced three million Allied soldiers in trenches across mud and barbed-wire entanglements in an area of the Western Front called No Man's Land. These trenches led into one another and were tied together in a city-like network. Soldiers named the trenches after their hometown streets. The soldiers themselves slept in holes dug alongside the trench walls or on cots in dugouts.

Rats often fed on unburied corpses. One officer, who had the use of a bed, recalled that "when he turned in that night, he heard a scuffling, shone his torch on the bed, and found two rats on his blankets tussling for the possession of a severed hand."

To keep warm, men burned whatever they could do without. Some made tea from water they had boiled by circulating it in the firing systems of machine guns. At night they raided enemy trenches and retrieved the wounded from No Man's Land. During the day, they went "over the top" to attack the other side. Many of them never made it more than a few feet before being brought down by machine-gun fire. Burdened with heavy equipment and entangled in their own barbed wire, they became perfect enemy targets. "Our dead were heaped on top of each other," said one British officer. "In places they were three to four deep."

German infantrymen on a fortified riverbank

Many referred to the war on the Western Front as "the sausage machine." One writer said "it was fed with live men, churned out corpses, and remained firmly screwed in place." Thousands lost their lives in such places along the front as the Somme, Verdun, Arras, Aisne, and Flanders.

At Verdun, the French and Germans fought the longest battle in history. After ten months and over half a million casualties, neither side had moved its front lines more than four miles. Some hills and villages changed hands as many as thirteen times a month.

On the Eastern Front the war was different. Not bogged down in trenches, German, Russian, and Austrian armies fought major battles from the Baltic to the Black Sea.

When Italy joined the Allies and attacked Austria in 1915, the war in Europe also had a southern front.

A Zeppelin downed by anti-aircraft guns off the coast of Britain

On all fronts, hydrogen-filled balloons were used to observe enemy positions. Later the Germans used their Zeppelin, a version of the balloon, to bomb French and British cities. Soon, however, airplanes replaced air balloons as the better vehicle for war.

The flimsy, poorly made planes, nicknamed "bird cages," barely stayed aloft. Pilots with little or no experience in flying risked their lives to observe the enemy and bring back vital information.

A British aircraft, the Bristol Fighter, in combat with a German aircraft

A few weeks into the war, however, a British plane flew over a German one and the pilots shot at each other with revolvers. Thereafter, planes were used for warfare. Within months, the "brave knights of the sky" were equipped with rifles and hand-held bombs. By 1915 machine guns were installed and pilots could shoot rapidly.

Without parachutes or protective armor, pilots were defenseless in the sky. When hit by gunfire, their planes became flaming coffins, carrying them to their graves.

Air ace Eddie Rickenbacker in his plane, June 22, 1918. Rickenbacker was the leading U.S. flier during World War I. He later became president of an airline company and also survived a plane crash in the Pacific Ocean.

By the middle of the war, the average flying life of a pilot was only three weeks. Some brave airmen, known as the Great Aces, became legends: America's Edward Rickenbacker, Germany's Manfred von Richthofen (nicknamed the "Red Baron"), Britain's Albert Ball, France's René Fonck, and Canada's William Bishop.

Above: German ace Baron Manfred von Richthofen, known as the Red Baron

Above right: The Red Baron's squadron

Right: Canadian ace William Bishop

The sinking of the British ship *Lusitania* in 1915

In February 1915 Germany announced that a war zone existed in the waters around the British Isles and that German U-boats (submarines) would be sinking any ships that entered it. Enraged by the announcement, President Wilson warned Germany that he would hold it responsible for any "injury to American property or lives."

Ignoring Wilson's message, German U-boats torpedoed the American tanker *Gulflight* on May 1, 1915. Some Americans died. Six days later they sank the British passenger ship *Lusitania*, killing 1,198 people—128 of them Americans. Still more Americans died when the French passenger steamer *Sussex* was torpedoed. When Wilson threatened to sever diplomatic relations with Germany the torpedo attacks stopped.

Bayonet drill in an American training camp

Outraged Americans began calling for U.S. intervention in the war. Many agreed with a New York minister that "it is getting to be too much to ask America to keep out when Americans are drowned as part of a European war." Wilson, yielding to the pressure, finally pushed for a program of preparedness. This meant increasing the size of the army and navy, establishing officers' training camps, and constructing new ships. Meanwhile, he continued to work for a peaceful settlement of the war. And he looked for someone to fill the loneliness he felt since Ellen's death.

President Wilson and Edith Galt at the 1915 World Series

In March he met Edith Bolling Galt at the White House. She was having tea with Helen Bones, Ellen's personal secretary and cousin. The president was instantly attracted to the charming, well-educated widow. Over the next few months they saw each other several times. With Ellen gone and two of his daughters married, Wilson needed someone with whom he could talk and share the weight of his lonely job. Edith filled those needs well. On December 18, 1915, less than a year after Ellen had died, Woodrow married Edith at her home in Washington, D.C. She was forty-three and he was a few days short of being fifty-nine.

Woodrow and Edith at the White House after their marriage

Immediately Edith became a warm and gracious First Lady, presiding over affairs in the White House. As Woodrow's closest assistant, she discussed political issues with him and read and typed his speeches. Trusting her to decode messages that came from abroad, Woodrow also had her translate them back into coded messages for his reply.

With Edith at his side and his personal life back in order, Woodrow was better able to face the issues of the war. The push for U.S. involvement was growing, and the 1916 presidential election was rapidly approaching.

This time, Wilson had a successful record to his credit and a slogan that attracted votes—"He Kept Us Out of War." By a narrow margin, he was reelected.

Trying again to negotiate peace in Europe, Wilson delivered his famous "Peace without Victory" speech to Congress on January 22, 1917. In it he pleaded that the end of the war "be a peace without victory. . . . Victory would mean peace forced upon the loser," he said. "Only a peace between equals [would] last." But at the same time Wilson was negotiating for peace, Germany was desperately trying to win the war.

On January 31, 1917, Germany resumed its submarine warfare. Three days later, Wilson broke diplomatic relations with Germany.

Late in February, the British intercepted a note from the German foreign minister Arthur Zimmermann to the German minister in Mexico City. In it Zimmermann urged his minister to get Mexico to declare war on the United States. In return, Mexico would be given back New Mexico, Arizona, and Texas after Germany won the war.

Next, four unarmed American merchant ships were sunk, with a loss of thirty-six lives. This brazen act settled most doubts about getting into the war, except for Wilson's. After wrestling with his decision for days, he finally concluded that the United States could not stand for continued German aggression. On April 2, 1917, before a joint session of Congress, he called the actions of Germany "nothing less than war against the government and people of the United States." He asked Congress to accept the state of war that was "thrust" upon them.

Wilson addressing Congress on April 2, 1917, urging a declaration of war

"We are glad . . . to fight thus for the ultimate peace of the world," he said, "and for the liberation of its peoples, the German peoples included; for the rights of nations great and small and the privilege of men everywhere to choose their way of life. . . . The world must be made safe for democracy. . . . It is a fearful thing to lead this great peaceful people into war," he admitted. "But the right is more precious than peace and we shall fight for the things which we have always carried nearest our hearts."

On April 6, 1917, Congress voted to declare war. The president, carrying on his shoulders the full responsibility for the decision, signed the document on the afternoon of April 7. Minutes later, news of the event was carried around the world.

75

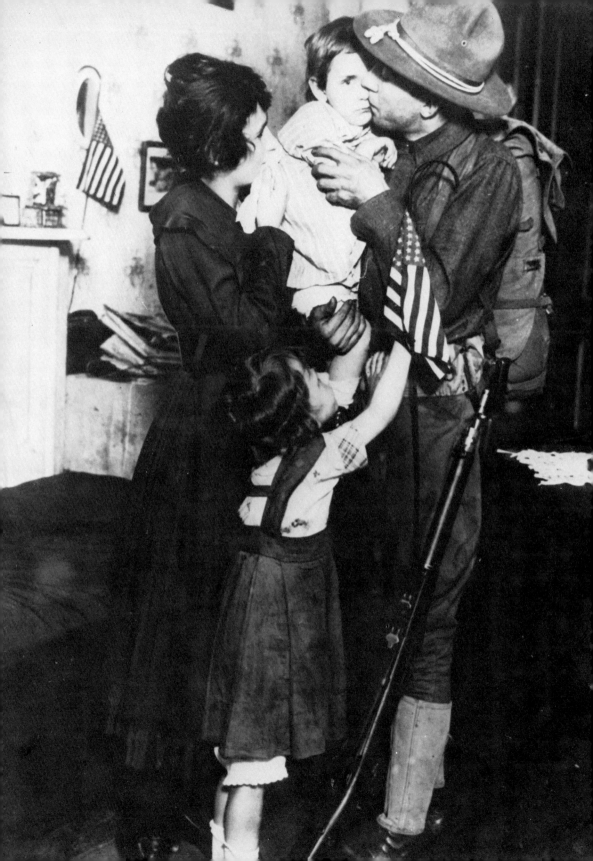

Chapter 9

The Yanks Are Coming!

"Over there, over there,
Send the word, send the word, over there
That the yanks are coming, the yanks are coming
The drum's rum tumming everywhere.
So prepare, say a prayer, send the word,
send the word to beware.

We'll be over, we're coming over
and we won't come back till it's over over there."

—George M. Cohan

On a balmy June day in 1917, relatives and friends of the American First Army cheered as a ship, carrying the first American soldiers to fight in Europe, pulled out of port. Final refrains of the song they were singing, George M. Cohan's "Over There," trailed behind them and slowly drifted out to sea.

Enormous changes had taken place in the United States before the first troops left for Europe. First, a Selective Service Act was passed, drafting men between the ages of twenty-one and thirty. Next, farmers were told to produce more food, and factories began operating around the clock to manufacture food, uniforms, and war equipment.

Opposite page: Private T. P. Laughlin of the
69th Infantry saying farewell to his family

I WANT YOU
FOR U.S. ARMY
NEAREST RECRUITING STATION

Left: A recruitment poster

Below: Women factory workers producing wartime materiel

General Pershing (facing ahead) making plans for maneuvers in France

President Wilson set up special boards to regulate industry and transportation and put Herbert Hoover in charge of a nationwide rationing program to conserve food and fuel. Soon Americans were "Hooverizing" to win the war, arranging their lives around "meatless days," "sweetless days," and "heatless days."

By the time the first American troops arrived in France, it was the fourth year of the war. Commanded by General John J. Pershing, Americans fought as separate units in thirteen major operations. Over a period of eighteen months, they turned back the Germans at Cantigny, Château-Thierry, Belleau Wood, the Marne, and St.-Mihiel. After fighting their way through a German stronghold in the Argonne Forest in September 1918, the tide of the war turned. The enemy began to crumble.

Signing the armistice of 1918 aboard a train

Bulgaria surrendered in September, the Ottoman Empire in October, and Austria-Hungary in November. Germany was left in a desperate situation. When its navy mutinied and its ruler abdicated, the nation called for a cease-fire. On November 11, 1918, Germany signed an armistice with the Allies.

Word filtered down to the troops that war would end at 11:00 that morning. Some troops stopped fighting and waited, hoping the rumor was true. Others fought to the last minute. When news of the armistice became official,

American soldiers in France celebrate the news of the German surrender.

the guns stopped and silence fell over the Western Front. Nearly ten million people were dead and over twenty million were left wounded. Over 116,000 Americans had given their lives.

President Wilson had received word of the armistice at 3:00 A.M. Hours later he broadcast the news to the anxious American public. "My fellow countrymen," he said, "the armistice was signed this morning. Everything for which America fought has been accomplished. It will now be our fortunate duty to assist . . . in the establishment of just democracy throughout the world."

Chapter 10

Victory without Peace

Among the many issues facing President Wilson after the war was the peace conference being held in Paris, France. He had given a lot of thought to the kind of settlement that would bring about a lasting peace. It was all outlined in the Fourteen Points peace plan he had proposed in January 1918.

The first thirteen points proposed several measures: open peace agreements with no secret dealings, freedom of the seas in peace and in war, removal of trade barriers, reduction of arms, fair adjustment of lands claimed as colonies, evacuation of German troops from invaded territories, and independence for Poland. The fourteenth point called for a League of Nations, which would protect any nation that was attacked by another.

All the countries involved in the war were aware of Wilson's Fourteen Points, but many opposed them. They wanted to maintain their armies, change the boundaries of defeated countries, and punish Germany severely.

Opposite page: Wilson on his sixty-fifth
birthday, December 29, 1921

The "Big Four" (seated, left to right): Orlando, Lloyd George, Clemenceau, and Wilson

Believing that only he could persuade leaders to adopt his peace plan, Wilson decided to go to Paris himself to lead the American Peace Commission. He, Edith, and several advisers boarded the *George Washington* and sailed for France on December 4, 1918. Ten days later they arrived there, greeted by a jubilant crowd.

At the peace conference delegates from twenty-seven nations had come to decide the fate of the Central Powers. To speed up the peace process, four leaders were chosen to lead the delegates. The Big Four, as they became known, were Premier Georges Clemenceau of France, Prime Minister David Lloyd George of Great Britain, Premier Vittorio Orlando of Italy, and Woodrow Wilson.

Wilson opened the second general session on January 25, 1919, with an exciting speech, urging the group to accept the League of Nations as part of the peace treaty. "It was a great moment in history," Edith Wilson commented, "as he stood there—slender, calm, and powerful in his argument—I seemed to see the people of all depressed countries—men, women and little children—crowded round and waiting upon his words."

Wilson's words were persuasive. The League of Nations was approved as Section I of the peace treaty. Pleased by the outcome, Wilson left Colonel House in Paris to act in his behalf, and returned to the United States to attend the final session of Congress.

When he returned to Paris in the middle of March, he learned that opponents of the League of Nations had managed to have it omitted from the peace treaty. Shocked and angry, Wilson worked to get it reinstated.

After days of long and tedious negotiations, the Big Four presented their results. The terms of the document, later called the Versailles Treaty, disappointed Wilson. He had obtained only part of the treaty provisions he wanted. In order to win support for the League, he had to compromise other issues.

In the treaty, Germany was blamed for the war. It was held responsible for $32 billion in war damages. It had to surrender a large portion of its merchant and fishing fleets and drastically reduce its army and navy. Finally Austria, Czechoslovakia, Yugoslavia, and Poland became independent countries. But the treaty also contained an agreement for a League of Nations.

Wilson returning to the United States from the Versailles peace conference

On June 28, 1919, representatives of the Allied countries and Germany signed the treaty in Versailles. Separate treaties were made with the other Central Powers. Thus the peace settlements officially came to a close.

When Wilson returned to the United States to get Senate approval for the peace treaty, he met with strong opposition. The first section of the Versailles Treaty provided for the establishment of a League of Nations, and some congressmen objected to it. They believed that, as a member of the League of Nations, the United States would be obligated to help solve world problems. U.S. involvement in

World War I had led many of them to believe that America should now stay away from foreign entanglements.

Knowing that Senate opposition to the treaty might kill its chances of passing, Wilson decided to take his request directly to the American people. Although feeling ill ever since the peace conference in Paris, Wilson began a speaking tour of the West. Despite his doctor's warning, Wilson left Washington by train on the third of September. For the next three weeks he gave two or three speeches a day, explaining the urgency of accepting the League of Nations. "This treaty is unique in the history of mankind," he told his listeners, "because the center of it is the redemption of weak nations. There never was a congress of nations before that considered the rights of those who could not enforce their rights."

By the time Wilson's train reached Pueblo, Colorado, on September 25, he was exhausted. Ignoring his fatigue, he delivered a rousing speech to the excited crowd. Shortly afterwards he collapsed from a nervous breakdown. The tour was cancelled and Wilson was brought back to Washington, D.C., where he was confined to his bed.

On October 2, Edith walked into the president's room and found him sitting on the edge of his bed, his left hand limp at his side. "I have no feeling in that hand," he told her. "Will you rub it?"

Immediately, Edith went for the doctor. When they returned, Woodrow was unconscious on the floor. He had suffered a stroke. After that, he was never physically well again. For the remaining months of his term in office, Edith and his cabinet members handled his affairs.

In March 1920 the Senate voted 49 to 35 against ratification of the Treaty of Versailles. In 1921 the United States signed a separate peace treaty with Germany, but it never joined the League of Nations. For Wilson, the defeat was a crushing blow. Although he was awarded the Nobel Peace Prize in December 1920 for his work on the League of Nations and the peace agreement, he could never accept the Senate's rejection of the treaty.

Wilson's physical condition improved enough to allow him to participate in the inauguration of Warren G. Harding, twenty-ninth president of the United States. Afterwards he and Edith moved to 2340 S Street in Washington. Among the many possessions they brought there was Woodrow's bookcase from Princeton—the one he had purchased with the first money he had ever earned—and his library of eight thousand books.

Shortly after retiring, Wilson formed a law partnership. But because of his health he was never able to practice, and the partnership was dissolved. Occasionally he made public appearances, and with Edith's help he wrote a short article. But he had lost his strength of purpose.

On February 3, 1924, Woodrow Wilson died quietly in his sleep. He had given himself completely to the cause of peace, believing to the end that the future would prove him right about the League of Nations.

As Wilson had told a group of friends outside his home on Armistice Day in 1923: "I am not one of those who have the least anxiety about the triumph of the principles I have stood for. . . . That we shall prevail is as sure as that God reigns."

Chronology of American History

(Shaded area covers events in Woodrow Wilson's lifetime.)

About A.D. 982—Eric the Red, born in Norway, reaches Greenland in one of the first European voyages to North America.

About 1000—Leif Ericson (Eric the Red's son) leads what is thought to be the first European expedition to mainland North America; Leif probably lands in Canada.

1492—Christopher Columbus, seeking a sea route from Spain to the Far East, discovers the New World.

1497—John Cabot reaches Canada in the first English voyage to North America.

1513—Ponce de Léon explores Florida in search of the fabled Fountain of Youth.

1519-1521—Hernando Cortés of Spain conquers Mexico.

1534—French explorers led by Jacques Cartier enter the Gulf of St. Lawrence in Canada.

1540—Spanish explorer Francisco Coronado begins exploring the American Southwest, seeking the riches of the mythical Seven Cities of Cibola.

1565—St. Augustine, Florida, the first permanent European town in what is now the United States, is founded by the Spanish.

1607—Jamestown, Virginia, is founded, the first permanent English town in the present-day U.S.

1608—Frenchman Samuel de Champlain founds the village of Quebec, Canada.

1609—Henry Hudson explores the eastern coast of present-day U.S. for the Netherlands; the Dutch then claim parts of New York, New Jersey, Delaware, and Connecticut and name the area New Netherland.

1619—The English colonies' first shipment of black slaves arrives in Jamestown.

1620—English Pilgrims found Massachusetts' first permanent town at Plymouth.

1621—Massachusetts Pilgrims and Indians hold the famous first Thanksgiving feast in colonial America.

1623—Colonization of New Hampshire is begun by the English.

1624—Colonization of present-day New York State is begun by the Dutch at Fort Orange (Albany).

1625—The Dutch start building New Amsterdam (now New York City).

1630—The town of Boston, Massachusetts, is founded by the English Puritans.

1633—Colonization of Connecticut is begun by the English.

1634—Colonization of Maryland is begun by the English.

1636—Harvard, the colonies' first college, is founded in Massachusetts. Rhode Island colonization begins when Englishman Roger Williams founds Providence.

1638—Delaware colonization begins as Swedes build Fort Christina at present-day Wilmington.

1640—Stephen Daye of Cambridge, Massachusetts prints *The Bay Psalm Book*, the first English-language book published in what is now the U.S.

1643—Swedish settlers begin colonizing Pennsylvania.

About 1650—North Carolina is colonized by Virginia settlers.

1660—New Jersey colonization is begun by the Dutch at present-day Jersey City.

1670—South Carolina colonization is begun by the English near Charleston.

1673—Jacques Marquette and Louis Jolliet explore the upper Mississippi River for France.

1682—Philadelphia, Pennsylvania, is settled. La Salle explores Mississippi River all the way to its mouth in Louisiana and claims the whole Mississippi Valley for France.

1693—College of William and Mary is founded in Williamsburg, Virginia.

1700—Colonial population is about 250,000.

1703—Benjamin Franklin is born in Boston.

1732—George Washington, first president of the U.S., is born in Westmoreland County, Virginia.

1733—James Oglethorpe founds Savannah, Georgia; Georgia is established as the thirteenth colony.

1735—John Adams, second president of the U.S., is born in Braintree, Massachusetts.

1737—William Byrd founds Richmond, Virginia.

1738—British troops are sent to Georgia over border dispute with Spain.

1739—Black insurrection takes place in South Carolina.

1740—English Parliament passes act allowing naturalization of immigrants to American colonies after seven-year residence.

1743—Thomas Jefferson is born in Albemarle County, Virginia. Benjamin Franklin retires at age thirty-seven to devote himself to scientific inquiries and public service.

1744—King George's War begins; France joins war effort against England.

1745—During King George's War, France raids settlements in Maine and New York.

1747—Classes begin at Princeton College in New Jersey.

1748—The Treaty of Aix-la-Chapelle concludes King George's War.

1749—Parliament legally recognizes slavery in colonies and the inauguration of the plantation system in the South. George Washington becomes the surveyor for Culpepper County in Virginia.

1750—Thomas Walker passes through and names Cumberland Gap on his way toward Kentucky region. Colonial population is about 1,200,000.

1751—James Madison, fourth president of the U.S., is born in Port Conway, Virginia. English Parliament passes Currency Act, banning New England colonies from issuing paper money. George Washington travels to Barbados.

1752—Pennsylvania Hospital, the first general hospital in the colonies, is founded in Philadelphia. Benjamin Franklin uses a kite in a thunderstorm to demonstrate that lightning is a form of electricity.

1753—George Washington delivers command that the French withdraw from the Ohio River Valley; French disregard the demand. Colonial population is about 1,328,000.

1754—French and Indian War begins (extends to Europe as the Seven Years' War). Washington surrenders at Fort Necessity.

1755—French and Indians ambush Braddock. Washington becomes commander of Virginia troops.

1756—England declares war on France.

1758—James Monroe, fifth president of the U.S., is born in Westmoreland County, Virginia.

1759—Cherokee Indian war begins in southern colonies; hostilities extend to 1761. George Washington marries Martha Dandridge Custis.

1760—George III becomes king of England. Colonial population is about 1,600,000.

1762—England declares war on Spain.

1763—Treaty of Paris concludes the French and Indian War and the Seven Years' War. England gains Canada and most other French lands east of the Mississippi River.

1764—British pass the Sugar Act to gain tax money from the colonists. The issue of taxation without representation is first introduced in Boston. John Adams marries Abigail Smith.

1765—Stamp Act goes into effect in the colonies. Business virtually stops as almost all colonists refuse to use the stamps.

1766—British repeal the Stamp Act.

1767—John Quincy Adams, sixth president of the U.S. and son of second president John Adams, is born in Braintree, Massachusetts. Andrew Jackson, seventh president of the U.S., is born in Waxhaw settlement, South Carolina.

1769—Daniel Boone sights the Kentucky Territory.

1770—In the Boston Massacre, British soldiers kill five colonists and injure six. Townshend Acts are repealed, thus eliminating all duties on imports to the colonies except tea.

1771—Benjamin Franklin begins his autobiography, a work that he will never complete. The North Carolina assembly passes the "Bloody Act," which makes rioters guilty of treason.

1772—Samuel Adams rouses colonists to consider British threats to self-government.

1773—English Parliament passes the Tea Act. Colonists dressed as Mohawk Indians board British tea ships and toss 342 casks of tea into the water in what becomes known as the Boston Tea Party. William Henry Harrison is born in Charles City County, Virginia.

1774—British close the port of Boston to punish the city for the Boston Tea Party. First Continental Congress convenes in Philadelphia.

1775—American Revolution begins with battles of Lexington and Concord, Massachusetts. Second Continental Congress opens in Philadelphia. George Washington becomes commander-in-chief of the Continental army.

1776—Declaration of Independence is adopted on July 4.

1777—Congress adopts the American flag with thirteen stars and thirteen stripes. John Adams is sent to France to negotiate peace treaty.

1778—France declares war against Great Britain and becomes U.S. ally.

1779—British surrender to Americans at Vincennes. Thomas Jefferson is elected governor of Virginia. James Madison is elected to the Continental Congress.

1780—Benedict Arnold, first American traitor, defects to the British.

1781—Articles of Confederation go into effect. Cornwallis surrenders to George Washington at Yorktown, ending the American Revolution.

1782—American commissioners, including John Adams, sign peace treaty with British in Paris. Thomas Jefferson's wife, Martha, dies. Martin Van Buren is born in Kinderhook, New York.

1784—Zachary Taylor is born near Barboursville, Virginia.

1785—Congress adopts the dollar as the unit of currency. John Adams is made minister to Great Britain. Thomas Jefferson is appointed minister to France.

1786—Shays's Rebellion begins in Massachusetts.

1787—Constitutional Convention assembles in Philadelphia, with George Washington presiding; U.S. Constitution is adopted. Delaware, New Jersey, and Pennsylvania become states.

1788—Virginia, South Carolina, New York, Connecticut, New Hampshire, Maryland, and Massachusetts become states. U.S. Constitution is ratified. New York City is declared U.S. capital.

1789—Presidential electors elect George Washington and John Adams as first president and vice-president. Thomas Jefferson is appointed secretary of state. North Carolina becomes a state. French Revolution begins.

1790—Supreme Court meets for the first time. Rhode Island becomes a state. First national census in the U.S. counts 3,929,214 persons. John Tyler is born in Charles City County, Virginia.

1791—Vermont enters the Union. U.S. Bill of Rights, the first ten amendments to the Constitution, goes into effect. District of Columbia is established. James Buchanan is born in Stony Batter, Pennsylvania.

1792—Thomas Paine publishes *The Rights of Man*. Kentucky becomes a state. Two political parties are formed in the U.S., Federalist and Republican. Washington is elected to a second term, with Adams as vice-president.

1793—War between France and Britain begins; U.S. declares neutrality. Eli Whitney invents the cotton gin; cotton production and slave labor increase in the South.

1794—Eleventh Amendment to the Constitution is passed, limiting federal courts' power. "Whiskey Rebellion" in Pennsylvania protests federal whiskey tax. James Madison marries Dolley Payne Todd.

1795—George Washington signs the Jay Treaty with Great Britain. Treaty of San Lorenzo, between U.S. and Spain, settles Florida boundary and gives U.S. right to navigate the Mississippi. James Polk is born near Pineville, North Carolina.

1796—Tennessee enters the Union. Washington gives his Farewell Address, refusing a third presidential term. John Adams is elected president and Thomas Jefferson vice-president.

1797—Adams recommends defense measures against possible war with France. Napoleon Bonaparte and his army march against Austrians in Italy. U.S. population is about 4,900,000.

1798—Washington is named commander-in-chief of the U.S. Army. Department of the Navy is created. Alien and Sedition Acts are passed. Napoleon's troops invade Egypt and Switzerland.

1799—George Washington dies at Mount Vernon, New York. James Monroe is elected governor of Virginia. French Revolution ends. Napoleon becomes ruler of France.

1800—Thomas Jefferson and Aaron Burr tie for president. U.S. capital is moved from Philadelphia to Washington, D.C. The White House is built as presidents' home. Spain returns Louisiana to France. Millard Fillmore is born in Locke, New York.

1801—After thirty-six ballots, House of Representatives elects Thomas Jefferson president, making Burr vice-president. James Madison is named secretary of state.

1802—Congress abolishes excise taxes. U.S. Military Academy is founded at West Point, New York.

1803—Ohio enters the Union. Louisiana Purchase treaty is signed with France, greatly expanding U.S. territory.

1804—Twelfth Amendment to the Constitution rules that president and vice-president be elected separately. Alexander Hamilton is killed by Vice-President Aaron Burr in a duel. Orleans Territory is established. Napoleon crowns himself emperor of France. Franklin Pierce is born in Hillsborough Lower Village, New Hampshire.

1805—Thomas Jefferson begins his second term as president. Lewis and Clark expedition reaches the Pacific Ocean.

1806—Coinage of silver dollars is stopped; resumes in 1836.

1807—Aaron Burr is acquitted in treason trial. Embargo Act closes U.S. ports to trade.

1808—James Madison is elected president. Congress outlaws importing slaves from Africa. Andrew Johnson is born in Raleigh, North Carolina.

1809—Abraham Lincoln is born near Hodgenville, Kentucky.

1810—U.S. population is 7,240,000.

1811—William Henry Harrison defeats Indians at Tippecanoe. Monroe is named secretary of state.

1812—Louisiana becomes a state. U.S. declares war on Britain (War of 1812). James Madison is reelected president. Napoleon invades Russia.

1813—British forces take Fort Niagara and Buffalo, New York.

1814—Francis Scott Key writes "The Star-Spangled Banner." British troops burn much of Washington, D.C., including the White House. Treaty of Ghent ends War of 1812. James Monroe becomes secretary of war.

1815—Napoleon meets his final defeat at Battle of Waterloo.

1816—James Monroe is elected president. Indiana becomes a state.

1817—Mississippi becomes a state. Construction on Erie Canal begins.

1818—Illinois enters the Union. The present thirteen-stripe flag is adopted. Border between U.S. and Canada is agreed upon.

1819—Alabama becomes a state. U.S. purchases Florida from Spain. Thomas Jefferson establishes the University of Virginia.

1820—James Monroe is reelected. In the Missouri Compromise, Maine enters the Union as a free (non-slave) state.

1821—Missouri enters the Union as a slave state. Santa Fe Trail opens the American Southwest. Mexico declares independence from Spain. Napoleon Bonaparte dies.

1822—U.S. recognizes Mexico and Colombia. Liberia in Africa is founded as a home for freed slaves. Ulysses S. Grant is born in Point Pleasant, Ohio. Rutherford B. Hayes is born in Delaware, Ohio.

1823—Monroe Doctrine closes North and South America to European colonizing or invasion.

1824—House of Representatives elects John Quincy Adams president when none of the four candidates wins a majority in national election. Mexico becomes a republic.

1825—Erie Canal is opened. U.S. population is 11,300,000.

1826—Thomas Jefferson and John Adams both die on July 4, the fiftieth anniversary of the Declaration of Independence.

1828—Andrew Jackson is elected president. Tariff of Abominations is passed, cutting imports.

1829—James Madison attends Virginia's constitutional convention. Slavery is abolished in Mexico. Chester A. Arthur is born in Fairfield, Vermont.

1830—Indian Removal Act to resettle Indians west of the Mississippi is approved.

1831—James Monroe dies in New York City. James A. Garfield is born in Orange, Ohio. Cyrus McCormick develops his reaper.

1832—Andrew Jackson, nominated by the new Democratic Party, is reelected president.

1833—Britain abolishes slavery in its colonies. Benjamin Harrison is born in North Bend, Ohio.

1835—Federal government becomes debt-free for the first time.

1836—Martin Van Buren becomes president. Texas wins independence from Mexico. Arkansas joins the Union. James Madison dies at Montpelier, Virginia.

1837—Michigan enters the Union. U.S. population is 15,900,000. Grover Cleveland is born in Caldwell, New Jersey.

1840—William Henry Harrison is elected president.

1841—President Harrison dies in Washington, D.C., one month after inauguration. Vice-President John Tyler succeeds him.

1843—William McKinley is born in Niles, Ohio.

1844—James Knox Polk is elected president. Samuel Morse sends first telegraphic message.

1845—Texas and Florida become states. Potato famine in Ireland causes massive emigration from Ireland to U.S. Andrew Jackson dies near Nashville, Tennessee.

1846—Iowa enters the Union. War with Mexico begins.

1847—U.S. captures Mexico City.

1848—Zachary Taylor becomes president. Treaty of Guadalupe Hidalgo ends Mexico-U.S. war. Wisconsin becomes a state.

1849—James Polk dies in Nashville, Tennessee.

1850—President Taylor dies in Washington, D.C.; Vice-President Millard Fillmore succeeds him. California enters the Union, breaking tie between slave and free states.

1852—Franklin Pierce is elected president.

1853—Gadsden Purchase transfers Mexican territory to U.S.

1854—"War for Bleeding Kansas" is fought between slave and free states.

1855—Czar Nicholas I of Russia dies, succeeded by Alexander II.

1856—James Buchanan is elected president. In Massacre of Potawatomi Creek, Kansas-slavers are murdered by free-staters. Woodrow Wilson is born in Staunton, Pennsylvania.

1857—William Howard Taft is born in Cincinnati, Ohio.

1858—Minnesota enters the Union. Theodore Roosevelt is born in New York City.

1859—Oregon becomes a state.

1860—Abraham Lincoln is elected president; South Carolina secedes from the Union in protest.

1861—Arkansas, Tennessee, North Carolina, and Virginia secede. Kansas enters the Union as a free state. Civil War begins.

1862—Union forces capture Fort Henry, Roanoke Island, Fort Donelson, Jacksonville, and New Orleans; Union armies are defeated at the battles of Bull Run and Fredericksburg. Martin Van Buren dies in Kinderhook, New York. John Tyler dies near Charles City, Virginia.

1863—Lincoln issues Emancipation Proclamation: all slaves held in rebelling territories are declared free. West Virginia becomes a state.

1864—Abraham Lincoln is reelected. Nevada becomes a state.

1865—Lincoln is assassinated in Washington, D.C., and succeeded by Andrew Johnson. U.S. Civil War ends on May 26. Thirteenth Amendment abolishes slavery. Warren G. Harding is born in Blooming Grove, Ohio.

1867—Nebraska becomes a state. U.S. buys Alaska from Russia for $7,200,000. Reconstruction Acts are passed.

1868—President Johnson is impeached for violating Tenure of Office Act, but is acquitted by Senate. Ulysses S. Grant is elected president. Fourteenth Amendment prohibits voting discrimination. James Buchanan dies in Lancaster, Pennsylvania.

1869—Franklin Pierce dies in Concord, New Hampshire.

1870—Fifteenth Amendment gives blacks the right to vote.

1872—Grant is reelected over Horace Greeley. General Amnesty Act pardons ex-Confederates. Calvin Coolidge is born in Plymouth Notch, Vermont.

1874—Millard Fillmore dies in Buffalo, New York. Herbert Hoover is born in West Branch, Iowa.

1875—Andrew Johnson dies in Carter's Station, Tennessee.

1876—Colorado enters the Union. "Custer's last stand": he and his men are massacred by Sioux Indians at Little Big Horn, Montana.

1877—Rutherford B. Hayes is elected president as all disputed votes are awarded to him.

1880—James A. Garfield is elected president.

1881—President Garfield is assassinated and dies in Elberon, New Jersey. Vice-President Chester A. Arthur succeeds him.

1882—U.S. bans Chinese immigration. Franklin D. Roosevelt is born in Hyde Park, New York.

1885—Ulysses S. Grant dies in Mount McGregor, New York.

1886—Statue of Liberty is dedicated. Chester A. Arthur dies in New York City.

1888—Benjamin Harrison is elected president.

1889—North Dakota, South Dakota, Washington, and Montana become states.

1890—Dwight D. Eisenhower is born in Denison, Texas. Idaho and Wyoming become states.

1892—Grover Cleveland is elected president.

1893—Rutherford B. Hayes dies in Fremont, Ohio.

1896—William McKinley is elected president. Utah becomes a state.

1898—U.S. declares war on Spain over Cuba.

1899—Philippines demand independence from U.S.

1900—McKinley is reelected. Boxer Rebellion against foreigners in China begins.

1901—McKinley is assassinated by anarchist Leon Czolgosz in Buffalo, New York; Theodore Roosevelt becomes president. Benjamin Harrison dies in Indianapolis, Indiana.

1902—U.S. acquires perpetual control over Panama Canal.

1903—Alaskan frontier is settled.

1904—Russian-Japanese War breaks out. Theodore Roosevelt wins presidential election.

1905—Treaty of Portsmouth signed, ending Russian-Japanese War.

1906—U.S. troops occupy Cuba.

1907—President Roosevelt bars all Japanese immigration. Oklahoma enters the Union.

1908—William Howard Taft becomes president. Grover Cleveland dies in Princeton, New Jersey. Lyndon B. Johnson is born near Stonewall, Texas.

1909—NAACP is founded under W.E.B. DuBois

1910—China abolishes slavery.

1911—Chinese Revolution begins. Ronald Reagan is born in Tampico, Illinois.

1912—Woodrow Wilson is elected president. Arizona and New Mexico become states.

1913—Federal income tax is introduced in U.S. through the Sixteenth Amendment. Richard Nixon is born in Yorba Linda, California. Gerald Ford is born in Omaha, Nebraska.

1914—World War I begins.

1915—British liner *Lusitania* is sunk by German submarine.

1916—Wilson is reelected president.

1917—U.S. breaks diplomatic relations with Germany. Czar Nicholas of Russia abdicates as revolution begins. U.S. declares war on Austria-Hungary. John F. Kennedy is born in Brookline, Massachusetts.

1918—Wilson proclaims "Fourteen Points" as war aims. On November 11, armistice is signed between Allies and Germany.

1919—Eighteenth Amendment prohibits sale and manufacture of intoxicating liquors. Wilson presides over first League of Nations; wins Nobel Peace Prize. Theodore Roosevelt dies in Oyster Bay, New York.

1920—Nineteenth Amendment (women's suffrage) is passed. Warren Harding is elected president.

1921—Adolf Hitler's stormtroopers begin to terrorize political opponents.

1922—Irish Free State is established. Soviet states form USSR. Benito Mussolini forms Fascist government in Italy.

1923—President Harding dies in San Francisco, California; he is succeeded by Vice-President Calvin Coolidge.

1924—Coolidge is elected president. Woodrow Wilson dies in Washington, D.C. James Carter is born in Plains, Georgia.

1925—Hitler reorganizes Nazi Party and publishes first volume of *Mein Kampf.*

1926—Fascist youth organizations founded in Germany and Italy. Republic of Lebanon proclaimed.

1927—Stalin becomes Soviet dictator. Economic conference in Geneva attended by fifty-two nations.

1928—Herbert Hoover is elected president. U.S. and many other nations sign Kellogg-Briand pacts to outlaw war.

1929—Stock prices in New York crash on "Black Thursday"; the Great Depression begins.

1930—Bank of U.S. and its many branches close (most significant bank failure of the year). William Howard Taft dies in Washington, D.C.

1931—Emigration from U.S. exceeds immigration for first time as Depression deepens.

1932—Franklin D. Roosevelt wins presidential election in a Democratic landslide.

1933—First concentration camps are erected in Germany. U.S. recognizes USSR and resumes trade. Twenty-First Amendment repeals prohibition. Calvin Coolidge dies in Northampton, Massachusetts.

1934—Severe dust storms hit Plains states. President Roosevelt passes U.S. Social Security Act.

1936—Roosevelt is reelected. Spanish Civil War begins. Hitler and Mussolini form Rome-Berlin Axis.

1937—Roosevelt signs Neutrality Act.

1938—Roosevelt sends appeal to Hitler and Mussolini to settle European problems amicably.

1939—Germany takes over Czechoslovakia and invades Poland, starting World War II.

1940—Roosevelt is reelected for a third term.

1941—Japan bombs Pearl Harbor, U.S. declares war on Japan. Germany and Italy declare war on U.S.; U.S. then declares war on them.

1942—Allies agree not to make separate peace treaties with the enemies. U.S. government transfers more than 100,000 Nisei (Japanese-Americans) from west coast to inland concentration camps.

1943—Allied bombings of Germany begin.

1944—Roosevelt is reelected for a fourth term. Allied forces invade Normandy on D-Day.

1945—President Franklin D. Roosevelt dies in Warm Springs, Georgia; Vice-President Harry S. Truman succeeds him. Mussolini is killed; Hitler commits suicide. Germany surrenders. U.S. drops atomic bomb on Hiroshima; Japan surrenders: end of World War II.

1946—U.N. General Assembly holds its first session in London. Peace conference of twenty-one nations is held in Paris.

1947—Peace treaties are signed in Paris. "Cold War" is in full swing.

1948—U.S. passes Marshall Plan Act, providing $17 billion in aid for Europe. U.S. recognizes new nation of Israel. India and Pakistan become free of British rule. Truman is elected president.

1949—Republic of Eire is proclaimed in Dublin. Russia blocks land route access from Western Germany to Berlin; airlift begins. U.S., France, and Britain agree to merge their zones of occupation in West Germany. Apartheid program begins in South Africa.

1950—Riots in Johannesburg, South Africa, against apartheid. North Korea invades South Korea. U.N. forces land in South Korea and recapture Seoul.

1951—Twenty-Second Amendment limits president to two terms.

1952—Dwight D. Eisenhower resigns as supreme commander in Europe and is elected president.

1953—Stalin dies; struggle for power in Russia follows. Rosenbergs are executed for espionage.

1954—U.S. and Japan sign mutual defense agreement.

1955—Blacks in Montgomery, Alabama, boycott segregated bus lines.

1956—Eisenhower is reelected president. Soviet troops march into Hungary.

1957—U.S. agrees to withdraw ground forces from Japan. Russia launches first satellite, *Sputnik.*

1958—European Common Market comes into being. Alaska becomes the forty-ninth state. Fidel Castro begins war against Batista government in Cuba.

1959—Hawaii becomes fiftieth state. Castro becomes premier of Cuba. De Gaulle is proclaimed president of the Fifth Republic of France.

1960—Historic debates between Senator John F. Kennedy and Vice-President Richard Nixon are televised. Kennedy is elected president. Brezhnev becomes president of USSR.

1961—Berlin Wall is constructed. Kennedy and Khrushchev confer in Vienna. In Bay of Pigs incident, Cubans trained by CIA attempt to overthrow Castro.

1962—U.S. military council is established in South Vietnam.

1963—Riots and beatings by police and whites mark civil rights demonstrations in Birmingham, Alabama; 30,000 troops are called out, Martin Luther King, Jr., is arrested. Freedom marchers descend on Washington, D.C., to demonstrate. President Kennedy is assassinated in Dallas, Texas; Vice-President Lyndon B. Johnson is sworn in as president.

1964—U.S. aircraft bomb North Vietnam. Johnson is elected president. Herbert Hoover dies in New York City.

1965—U.S. combat troops arrive in South Vietnam.

1966—Thousands protest U.S. policy in Vietnam. National Guard quells race riots in Chicago.

1967—Six-Day War between Israel and Arab nations.

1968—Martin Luther King, Jr., is assassinated in Memphis, Tennessee. Senator Robert Kennedy is assassinated in Los Angeles. Riots and police brutality take place at Democratic National Convention in Chicago. Richard Nixon is elected president. Czechoslovakia is invaded by Soviet troops.

1969—Dwight D. Eisenhower dies in Washington, D.C. Hundreds of thousands of people in several U.S. cities demonstrate against Vietnam War.

1970—Four Vietnam War protesters are killed by National Guardsmen at Kent State University in Ohio.

1971—Twenty-Sixth Amendment allows eighteen-year-olds to vote.

1972—Nixon visits Communist China; is reelected president in near-record landslide. Watergate affair begins when five men are arrested in the Watergate hotel complex in Washington, D.C. Nixon announces resignations of aides Haldeman, Ehrlichman, and Dean and Attorney General Kleindienst as a result of Watergate-related charges. Harry S. Truman dies in Kansas City, Missouri.

1973—Vice-President Spiro Agnew resigns; Gerald Ford is named vice-president. Vietnam peace treaty is formally approved after nineteen months of negotiations. Lyndon B. Johnson dies in San Antonio, Texas.

1974—As a result of Watergate cover-up, impeachment is considered; Nixon resigns and Ford becomes president. Ford pardons Nixon and grants limited amnesty to Vietnam War draft evaders and military deserters.

1975—U.S. civilians are evacuated from Saigon, South Vietnam, as Communist forces complete takeover of South Vietnam.

1976—U.S. celebrates its Bicentennial. James Earl Carter becomes president.

1977—Carter pardons most Vietnam draft evaders, numbering some 10,000.

1980—Ronald Reagan is elected president.

1981—President Reagan is shot in the chest in assassination attempt. Sandra Day O'Connor is appointed first woman justice of the Supreme Court.

1983—U.S. troops invade island of Grenada.

1984—Reagan is reelected president. Democratic candidate Walter Mondale's running mate, Geraldine Ferraro, is the first woman selected for vice-president by a major U.S. political party.

1985—Soviet Communist Party secretary Konstantin Chernenko dies; Mikhail Gorbachev succeeds him. U.S. and Soviet officials discuss arms control in Geneva. Reagan and Gorbachev hold summit conference in Geneva. Racial tensions accelerate in South Africa.

1986—Space shuttle *Challenger* explodes shortly after takeoff; crew of seven dies. U.S. bombs bases in Libya. Corazon Aquino defeats Ferdinand Marcos in Philippine presidential election.

1987—Iraqi missile rips the U.S. frigate *Stark* in the Persian Gulf, killing thirty-seven American sailors. Congress holds hearings to investigate sale of U.S. arms to Iran to finance Nicaraguan *contra* movement.

Index

Page numbers in boldface type indicate illustrations.

About the Author

    Alice Osinski is a Chicago-based free-lance writer and photo researcher. She holds a B.A. in the Social Sciences, with special coursework in American Indian Studies. After teaching American Indian children for seven years in Pine Ridge, South Dakota, and Gallup, New Mexico, Ms. Osinski launched her career in writing. She has developed bicultural curricula for alternative school programs in South Dakota and New Mexico. Her articles and children's stories have appeared in textbooks for D.C. Heath and Open Court. She has written several books for Childrens Press, including *Andrew Jackson* and *Franklin D. Roosevelt* in the *Encyclopedia of Presidents* series.